Bus Dri[ver]

Written by Sue Barraclough
Photography by Chris Fairclough

W
FRANKLIN WATTS
LONDON•SYDNEY

This edition 2010

First published in 2006 by Franklin Watts
338 Euston Road, London NW1 3BH

Franklin Watts Australia
Level 17/207 Kent Street
Sydney NSW 2000

© 2006 Franklin Watts

Editor: Adrian Cole
Designer: Jemima Lumley
Art direction: Jonathan Hair
Photography: Chris Fairclough

The publisher wishes to thank Sally, Brian, Kate, David and Adam
at Arriva, and to Joyce for taking part

A CIP catalogue record for this book is available
from the British Library

ISBN 978 0 7496 9669 6

Printed in China

Franklin Watts is a division of Hachette Children's Books,
an Hachette UK company.
www.hachette.co.uk

Contents

I am a bus driver

My name is Sally. I am a bus driver. I spend most of my day picking up and dropping off passengers.

I start the day at a busy depot full of buses.
I wear a bright yellow waistcoat so I can
be seen as I walk across the depot.

Starting work

First, I go to see the inspector.
He gives me a bus number
and my duty rota.

Then I collect my cash box and my module. The module records lots of information. I put it into a machine so it is ready to use. I take the module with me to use on the bus.

Checking the bus

Before I set off, I have a list of things that
I must check on the bus. I check the
wheels, lights and emergency exits.

One of the wheel nuts is loose. I ask the mechanic to tighten it.

Getting ready

I place my bus
number in the
front window.

I put my module
into the ticket
machine. Then I fit
a new ticket roll.

I am on route 132. I type in the number, which appears on the front, back and sides of the bus. Then I can start the bus route.

If someone is waiting at a bus stop, they put out their hand to stop the bus. I pull into the bus stop to pick them up.

Some people show me
their bus passes. Other
people pay a fare and
I give them a ticket.

Getting on and off

Bus passengers ring the bell
when they want to get off.
I pull in at the next bus stop.

I press a button
to open the doors.

The doors open
to let passengers
on or off the bus.

I can lower the bus floor so that it is easier for people with pushchairs to get on and off.

There is also a special ramp so wheelchair users can get on and off.

On my route

Sometimes we travel very slowly, stopping at traffic lights and in queues of cars.

Some streets have special bus lanes. The bus can travel faster in a bus lane and pass by traffic queues.

When I have finished my route, I drive back to the depot. I check the bus for lost property. Then I park the bus so it can be cleaned.

I tip the fare money from my cash box into a machine. I put notes into a special slot. The machine counts all the money.

Later, all the money is sorted and checked in the cash office.

Cleaning and refuelling

When the bus arrives back at the depot, it is cleaned inside. The outside is cleaned in the bus wash.

The mechanic fills up the bus with fuel. He checks the engine, too. Now the bus is ready to go out in the morning.

Finishing work

At the end of the day, I hand in any lost property found on the bus. The inspector keeps a record of it.

I put my cash box and my module into my locker. Now it is time for me to go home.

Bus driving equipment

When I sit in the **driver's seat** I can reach everything I need easily.

A **module** records information about the number of people who get on the bus. It also records how much money is collected from them.

The **ticket machine** is at the front of the bus. It prints tickets for some passengers.

The **cash box** is kept under the ticket machine on the bus.

The **mirrors** are important for driving. They also help the driver to see the passengers.

Travelling safely on a bus

- When you are waiting at a bus stop, stand back from the road.

- If the bus has only one door, wait for people to get off before you get on.

- Always sit down or hold on tightly while the bus is moving.

- To get off at the next stop, press the button to ring the bell.

- If you are sitting down, wait until the bus has stopped before you get up.

- If you need to cross the road, follow the Green Cross Code: think, stop, look, listen, wait, arrive alive.

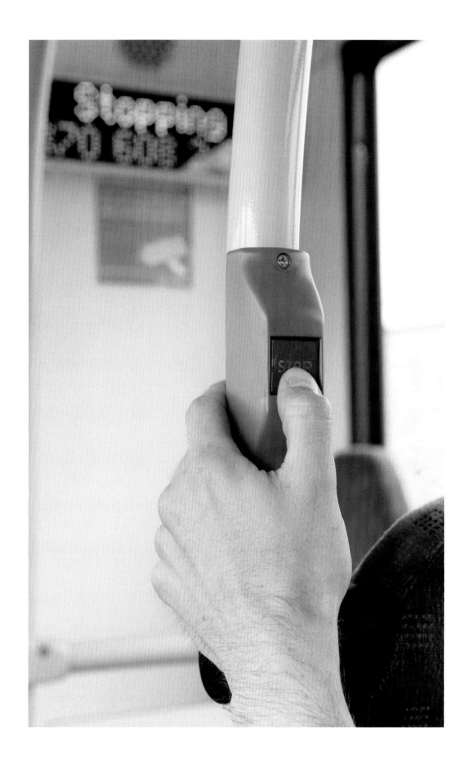

Glossary and index

bus route - the journey the bus takes from the place it starts to the place where it finishes. **Pages 13, 20**

cash box - a metal box used to store money from passengers' fares. **Pages 9, 21, 25, 27**

depot - a place where things are stored. **Pages 7, 20, 22**

duty rota - a list telling bus drivers when they have to work, and what bus routes they will drive on. **Page 8**

fare - the money paid by passengers to travel somewhere. **Pages 15, 21**

lost property - things that passengers leave behind by mistake. **Pages 20, 24**

module - a special card that slots into a ticket machine and records information. **Pages 9, 12, 25, 26**

ticket machine - the machine that prints out tickets for passengers. **Pages 12, 27**

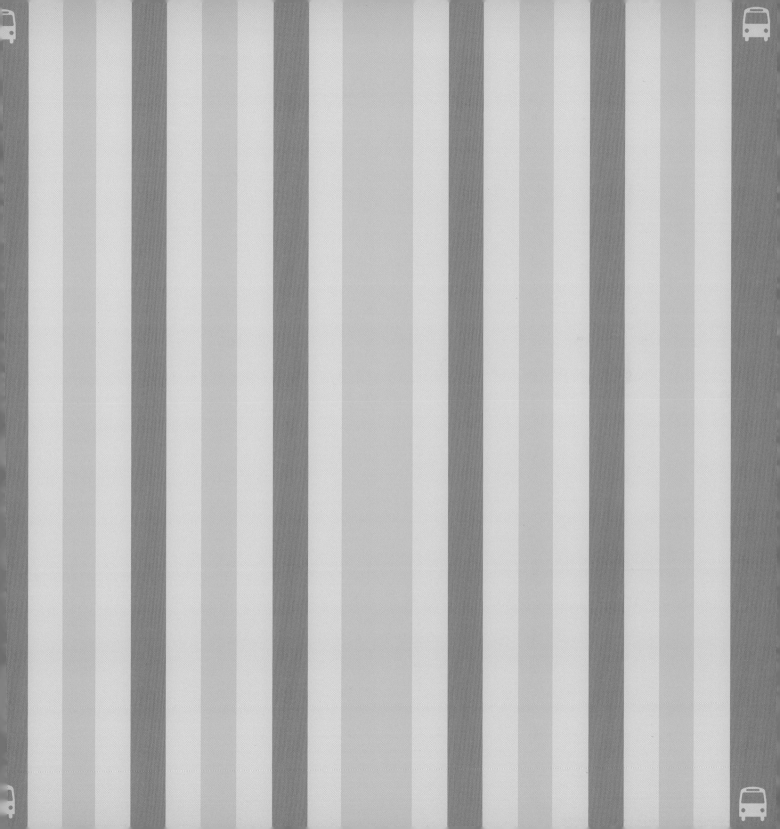

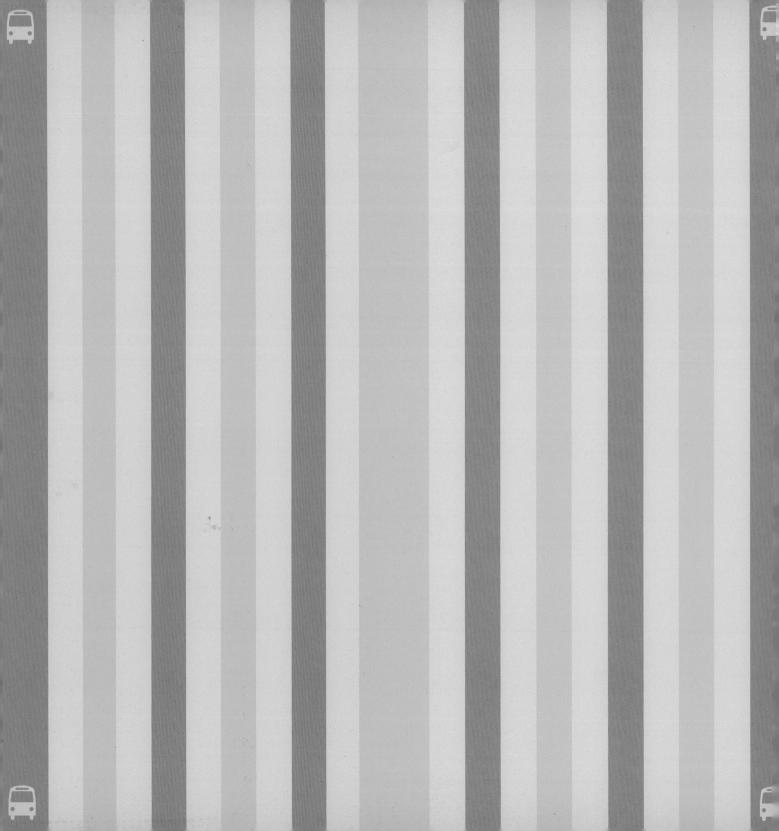